Hair Art

Written by
Daisy Hawkins

Hair can be a form of art.

You can go for all sorts of "looks".

She has a lob (that is, a long bob).

She has highlights too.

Highlights look good with a lob, but the foils are not a quick job!

She has a bun.

You might need to pop pins in a bun, to keep it high and tight.

Hair is not near the ears in this look.

Or you can part the hair and get lots of buns.

He has a quiff.

Forget pins! You need to fix a quiff with hair wax.

She has a buzz cut.

She can go for the no-hair look, or she can get a wig.

Wigs are good if you are keen on long hair, short hair, fair hair **and** dark hair.

With a wig, you can get a look for a bit, then go back to how it was.

He has a beard. Beard hair can be part of a look too.

For a sharp beard, you need to keep the chin high as you cut it.

Beards need shampoo and oil too.

Now that you are in my chair, will you go for hair that is art?